TABLE OF CONTENTS

1. Character Based Youth Financial Literacy Curriculum

2. <u>Patrick Puckle & Friends It's Best to Invest</u> Book Series

3. Curriculum in action sample pictures

(Patrick Puckle & Friends personal back stories can be learned about in Ben Popp's character counts lesson plans bundle book.)

CURRICULUM

Patrick Puckle and Friends say . . . . It's Best to Invest! You, too, can shoot for Excellence, be the Best you can be through hard work, and be Financially Secure!
Patrick Puckle and Friends say . . . . .
You, too, can accomplish your dreams by staying focused, showing initiative, understanding your skill-set, having integrity, being resilient, and delaying self-gratification!
Big Idea: Patrick Puckle and each of his Friends introduce the plans they put into practice daily in order to have a secure and sound financial future.
Patrick Puckle and each of his Friends want you to know that the tv you watch, the toys you play with, and the cars you drive would not be here without certain people who budget or invest their funds and faith on research and development to make these things.
Patrick says: It's important to know the difference between your needs and wants.
It's important to delay self-gratification so that you can save for really important things you may need or want.
<u>What should you do with all of your birthday money or your allowance? What does it mean to budget? What does it mean to deposit money? To withdraw money?</u>
It's important to understand what it means to invest some of your saved money and to understand what

investing is, who investors are, and what kinds of stock investments are made.

Patrick's Hands on Lesson

*First, show a $100. 00 bill inside a big birthday card! Have several jars with labels on how to **budget.** Put smaller $1.00 bills in the movie jar, new clothes jar, savings account jar, etc. Now, repeat if you become a cool teenager or an adult. Your budgeting practices remain the same. However, the labels change somewhat to : Electric bills, Water bills, Heating bills, Car payments, Gas weekly, etc.

1. Set up a row of empty cans with company stock label i.e. McDonalds, Toys R Us, Apple, Disney, Caterpillar Earth –Moving Equipment. (include a real or approximate price per/stock)

2. Give each student a colored strip of paper that matches the stock label.

3. Students can put in as many strips of paper into the company they want fully understanding they are now part owner of the company as well as understanding how much money they have invested.

4. Provide each student with a folded portfolio with a list of the canned companies. Students can color in how many stocks they have invested in each company. Explain the importance of a portfolio.

Mickey says: It is important to understand diversification when you invest. What is diversification? Think of a menu. Think of each part of a menu. Look at all of the Appetizers you can choose. Look at all of the Meat dishes. Look at all of the Seafood choices. Look at all of the Desserts. Diversification is just like a restaurant menu. One real example of diversification is investing in a Mutual Fund.

Mickey's Hands on Lesson
1. Show students a basket labeled "Mutual Fund" with real objects or visuals of products from different companies and manufacturers. Show students that when an investor invests in a mutual fund that there is a pool of diverse products and that is why it is such a safe and sure stock to have in your portfolio. Keep to Mickey's health theme with: Johnson & Johnson sunscreen, cotton balls, Q-tips, pictures of wheelchairs and canes, etc.

    Jini says: Because we live in a Global Economy and people from all around the world do business with one another, it is important to understand what the United States imports and exports. It is important to understand International Banking as well as what countries from around the world invest in. Finally, it is important to know what some forms of currency looks like in the world of international banking and business.

Jini's Hands on Lesson

1. Pass out bags of gold nuggets chewing gum. Show some fool's gold rocks from Lake Geneva or we can spray some blocks golden. Show some printed foreign currency.

2. Show a floor pie graph. Label the inside of each piece or wedge of pie with products we import i.e. petroleum from the Middle East, Diamonds from Africa, toys made in China. Show pie pieces with things the U.S. exports i.e. wheat, barley, oats and grains to places around the world that can't grow food, (put a basket of bread in this wedge of the circle), Caterpillar earth-moving equipment to all parts of the world (place small yellow excavators, bulldozers).

Nick says: Investing can be done with a company or an investor can trade by himself or herself daily. Day trading exists for investors who want to be completely in control of their decisions. Regardless of how the money is invested, Nick is grateful for investors who invest money in stocks called "Pharmaceuticals". These research and development companies make medicines for diseases such as cancer. Nick feels so thankful that investors poured some of their savings in these scientists so that they could buy the laboratory supplies they needed to study and manufacture new drugs for him. He used these new medicines and now he is cancer free!

Nick's Hands on Lesson

1. Hang up a clothesline in the classroom.
2. Hang up the parts of the body to represent each system: Neurological (brain and spinal chord), Respiratory (heart and lungs), Digestive (stomach and intestines), Circulatory (blood, heart), etc.
3. Under each picture, have a white lab coat with labels of the kind of money day traders and all other investors put their faith and money into such as: Football brain injuries like concussions

4. * If no investor put their $ into such research, there would be no cures!
5. Explain how the investors benefit from all of this: if a pharmaceutical company develops a new medicine or good drug to make people well, then the drug sells and the investors get a percentage of the money.

Chung and Pierre say: Many investors invest in the supplies and food ingredients that Chung and Pierre use to own and operate a restaurant. These supplies and food ingredients are called "Commodities". The types of commodities that can be invested in are the following: oil to cook with and to use as kitchen and restaurant fuel and energy, beef, grains, fish, as well as the means of transportation that are used to transport these important supplies to their restaurant such as planes, ships, and trucks.

Chung and Pierre's Hands on Lesson

1. Let's sort. Each student receives a plastic bag with words and pictures. Some words are the names of different subsectors that investors invest in such as: TRANSPORTATION, SEAFOOD, MEAT, FRUITS AND VEGETABLES . Chung and Pierre need to order from these categories.

2. Next, there are pictures or visuals inside each plastic bag that must be sorted and placed under the correct subsector headings. Ex: picture of poultry like turkeys, chickens, cows, and pigs go under the MEAT and pictures of apples, bananas, tomatoes, and lettuce go under FRUITS and VEGETABLES. Under TRANSPORTATION a student would put a truck that hauls apples from Michigan, or a ship with oil from Saudi Arabia.

Vocabulary to learn using Hands on Activities!

To invest
Investor
Investments
To deposit
To Withdraw
Needs
Wants
Mutual funds
Sectors/Sub-sectors
To budget

Patrick Puckle & Friends It's Best To Invest!
Money Basics!

Hey there I'm Patrick Puckle!, and I want to teach you kids the right way of investing! But first, we must go over some basics of money.

It all starts with our parents going to work for two weeks. After the two weeks of work, our moms and dads receive their paycheck. But what do parents do with their money after they get their check?

A parent first pays their bills like the heat, water, car or the gas bill. Once the bills are paid, the parent has a list of choices of what they can do with the rest of the money. This is called budgeting. They can keep the rest of the money for fast food, gas or other expenses, or the parent can put their left over money into their checking or savings account called a deposit.

A checking account is meant for money that is used often; like for unexpected bills. A savings account, is where money is put into monthly and never touched until the day they want to stop working called retirement. Most adults put part of their paycheck into their savings accounts so one day, when they don't have to work, they will have enough money to live without working.

Is that all someone can do with their money?
No. Actually, there are several places people can put their money. People can invest their money in stocks and real estate. In fact, you could invest in a sector like Health & Rehab. Remember, I'm the character who has the bad leg. And, the more people that invest in physical aids, for further research, the better I'll be able to move around.

Why do people invest? Investing is a way for a person to make more money, based off of how much money they put into the investment in the first place.

For example, people put their money into a company's stock. If you buy stock in a company, you own shares. A share of stock, is one small piece of a company that you own! And every investment you make, is put into what you call your portfolio.

But before someone puts their money where they think they'll get more money back later on, they must do their homework. Doing your homework means studying a company; making sure they are always truthful, grow money every year, and have good products or ideas that will make them money in the future! And in return, you are rewarded with extra money you never had before! All because you put your money and faith in the company.

There's two ways to study stocks. One, is is called fundamental analysis. Fundamental analysis is the study of the industry conditions, company's financial well- being, economy, and management.

And the second form is called technical analysis. Technical Analysis is more interested in price movements of a stock, rather than true value. Technical Analysis focuses on the study of companies charts and graphs, in order to predict how the stock will perform in the future.

But be careful, instead of putting all of your eggs in one basket, you need to invest your money in different sectors called diversification. An example would be to have stock in a toy company, your favorite food company, and your favorite car company. It is important to diversify because if the food, and toy companies do poorly, you have your car company stock to make up for it!

Once again, when people invest, it allows a company to use that investor's money, to do research and come up with better gadgets that make people's lives easier in the future!

Just think, without people investing, many companies, ideas, products, and medicines would have never came about! So the next time you or your parents find yourselves with extra money in your budgets, remember what I told you about the benefits of investing.

Patrick Puckle & Friends It's Best To Invest!
Trade Stocks!

Hey there, I'm Nick! And, I'd like to teach you kids more about investing than Patrick did!

First off, I love investing because it has helped my health get better, and never again will I be sick! I was only able to get better because of the investors who put their money in the medicine sector called Pharmaceuticals.

Remember, investors are the ones who give their money to a company, in hopes the company can use that money to create a product that can bring investors more cash in the future to reward their faith!

When you hear someone say "the stock market" they're not talking about a food stand. They are talking about a place where stocks are bought and sold every day! People can only invest for certain hours of the day according to the stock market's hours of operation.

The stock market is made up of sectors and subsectors. An example of a sector would be transports; which is trains, planes, trucks and ships. A subsector would be items that are transported by those ships such as food, drinks, money or tourists!

Remember, when you're investing you need to be diversified. That means you must have different stocks in different sectors. Examples of sectors are energy, tech, finance, services, health and retail. For example, if the transports sector is doing poorly, than the items being transported won't make any substantial gains either.

So keep in mind when your buying stocks, make sure you don't buy two of the same stocks that go hand in hand. For example, a car company who's sales aren't doing well, means that tire companies will more than likely be failing also.

Not only can you invest in stocks, you can invest in real estate! Real estate has to do with the buying and selling of land and the housing market. If someone doesn't feel safe putting their money into stocks because of the ups and downs of stock prices, they can invest their money into a house.

So like a stock, years down the road, the investor sells the house for more than he paid for it! But remember, real estate can be a burden if your not willing to sell in a poor economy, and it could take a toll on your patience.

Not only can you buy and hold stocks until they make you money, but you can trade stocks too! Stocks are traded all over the world, and in most countries!

If people don't want to wait a long time to get their money back from investing called long term investing, they can trade stocks by day, called day trading!

Day trading let's investors make quick money from their back and fourth buying and selling of stocks! But be careful if you trade stocks a lot, because if you do, at the end of the year you will have to pay money for your successful trading called capital gains tax.

Capital gains tax means any money that you made for the year, the government gets to take some money out of your account. So remember, the less you trade, the less money you will have to pay to the government at the end of the year! But if your stocks lose money, your tax advisor may be able to use your losses to lower your taxes called a deduction!

Keep in mind, that day trading is an art. You must do your homework ahead of time before choosing to buy a stock. Once in a while you may get lucky by buying a speculative stock. A speculative stock is a stock that is very risky, but you believe that the company will come out with a product that will soar the stock price higher in a short amount of time!

Just think, without people investing, many companies, ideas, products, and medicines would have never came about! Remember, not only did people's investments cure my illness, but having a diversified portfolio can be the precise prescription for a winning portfolio!

Patrick Puckle & Friends It's Best To Invest!
Keep Your Money!

Hello there, I'm Mickey! And I'm here to teach you how to keep the money you earned from investing!

I am a major fan of investing because it has helped me continue to play basketball and enhance my mobility! I was only able to move around again because of the investors who put their money in the Health and Rehab sector.

Remember, investors are the ones who give their money to a company, in hopes the company can use that money to create a product that can bring investors more cash in the future to reward their faith!

Building off of what Patrick and Nick taught us, I will teach you how to keep your money, and how adults plan for retirement using capital preservation investment types!

Many parents of ours plan for their retirement every day by living a certain way. Your parents set an age where they feel they can retire with enough money. So, in order to meet that goal, they must spend their money wisely. Some hire a financial advisor to help them plan for retirement.

That's where capital preservation investments come in to play. It's sounds like a scary word, but all capital preservation means is a way someone can keep the money they made and receive interest for a certain amount of years.

Interest is money placed in your investment account by the financial institution such as a bank or investment firm, that grows over the years into a big number!

One type of fund parents who want to retire put their money in, is called a mutual fund. A mutual fund is a group of stocks or assets placed into one fund. There are different types of funds: Aggressive, Value and Growth.

An aggressive investment means it is risky and is more focused on making the quick dollar in a short amount of time; which young folks tend to invest in. A growth investment means it grows at a steady rate for a number of years; which requires much patience. A value investment is a stock that is selling for a price much lower than it should be.

Another type of investment parents would invest in are called bonds. Bonds are offered by the government and companies. What is a bond? When people invest in bonds, they pay a certain amount of money, with a promise of more money in a certain amount of time. Who should own bonds? People entering retirement ages, because owning stocks is to risky for their age and money.

To help parents plan for their retirement, most of their workplaces offer 401K's. A 401K is savings account in a way, because parents put money into the 401K every year.

The money parents put into their 401K's, is sometimes matched by their employers. But be careful, 401K's can be dangerous if the business or company they work for goes out of business! If that happens, there is a great chance that all of the money will be lost.

It's much better to invest outside of your company, with a similar investment called a Roth IRA. A Roth IRA is similar to a 401K in terms of money being placed into the fund every year, and withdrawn during retirement; usually growing tax deferred. Tax deferred means your money grows with no taxes taken out from it until a set time. And just like a 401K, A Roth IRA has penalties for pulling your money out of the fund before the set date.

We can take away from this, that youngsters like us should invest more in stocks, and other aggressive investments because of our age and time window to work. On the other hand, older people should focus on preserving their money by investing in bonds, mutual funds, and Roth IRA's.

Just think, without people investing, many companies, ideas, products, and medicines would have never came about! Plus, many people would have never been able to retire!

INTERNATIONAL TRADING!

WRITTEN & ILLUSTRATED
BY BEN POPP

Patrick Puckle & Friends It's Best To Invest!
International Trading

Welcome, I'm Jini! And I'm here to teach you about international trading! Coming from the Middle East, I sure know my facts when it comes to international business transactions.

I am a major fan of overseas investing because it has helped countries get along with each other through the buying and selling of each others goods!

Why do people invest in foreign? For example, when the United States's economy is doing poorly, some Americans invest in other countries because their economy is healthy.

In the Middle East, our major export is oil. An export is a good that a country sends to the buying country that doesn't have that resource or great amounts of.

An example of an import, would be the United States buying oil from the Middle East.

Import and export prices become expensive when one country raises the price of their goods; due to bad crops, supply or making up for lost profits.

Oil's role in our everyday lives like, driving, eating, cutting the grass, and building wouldn't be possible if no one invested!

Another form of international investing is trading currencies! Trading currencies simply is the conversion of different countries money in different economies. For example, if China's Yen is doing poorly, some Chinese investors would switch their Yen into United States dollars; should the United States economy is doing well.

Another investment countries participate in, is the buying and selling of gold. In bad markets, gold is worth more than money.

How can people invest in gold? People can invest directly in a company who mines gold, or they can invest in an ETF that tracks gold. An ETF is an exchange-traded fund that follows a handful of companies for a particular sector.

For example, a gold ETF would track a list of several mining companies all in one fund. Usually older people tend to invest in gold because gold can be used as a hedge against market downturns. But in the end, gold never has the long-term value of money.

Keep in mind that without investors, oil wouldn't have been found without funding for research and development within companies! So the next time you or your parents have extra money in your budgets, be sure to consider overseas investing. Because this international investment may be a goldmine for your portfolio!

Patrick Puckle & Friends It's Best To Invest!
Commodities!

Hey everyone, we're Chung & Pierre! And we want to teach you another thing people invest in; commodities!

And without investors, Pierre and I would never have been given the opportunity to cook and open a restaurant!

Having a basketful of background knowledge on food, we can teach you how the commodities trade works.

It sounds like a scary word, but all a commodity is, is a marketable item made and transported to satisfy wants or needs. Satisfying needs and wants is called economics.

For example, in the Midwest there is no ocean nearby. So if people want to eat fish, they import fish from places near a sea. Because people in the Midwest like fish so much, places who export fish raise the price according to how much the Midwest people want the fish.

Some examples of commodities are beef, grain, oil and even gas! We mention oil and gas, because the two let us start up our grill and cook!

Many commodities are traded every day in the stock market that are within the food sector!

Remember, when people import food, they are paying the price for what the sellers want for the good. When people export, they are selling a product that they chose the price for.

Besides being eaten, a commodity like corn is also used for alternative energy! Plus, on the farm where the corn is grown, are wind turbines that help generate energy naturally!

Import and export are determined by the laws of supply and demand. For example, if farmers don't have good corn crops this season, the price of the corn will rise because of the small amounts the farm produced.

If people buy corn that year, they'll know why corn is more expensive due to simple supply and demand. In other words, if the farmers' supply is limited due to a poor harvest, and the demand or the desire to purchase large amounts of corn is great, then the price of the corn is going to be high.

So, the reason why the corn crop is so expensive, is because the farmer needs to cover his losses due to the poor harvest.

Just think, without investors, many business loans, alternative energy and restaurants would not have come to life! So remember, the next time you or your parents have any extra money in your budgets, the best way to grow your money is by investing.

And, part of being diversified means investing in commodities, which may be the next best thing on your plate and your portfolio.

Curriculum in action sample pictures

Money Basics

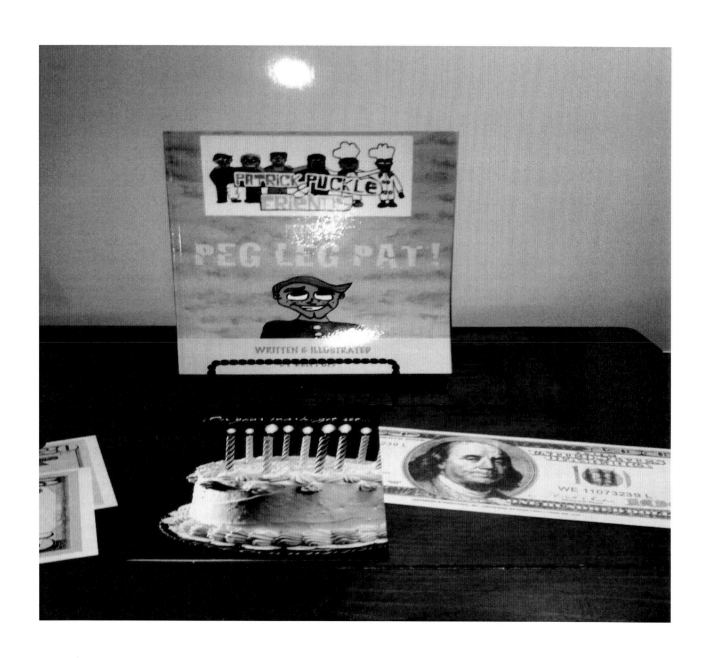

Money Basics

Trade Stocks

Keep Your Money

Keep Your Money

International Trading

International Trading

International Trading

Commodities

Commodities

Made in United States
North Haven, CT
07 July 2022